Christ *Beside* Me, Christ *Within* Me

CELTIC BLESSINGS

BETH A. RICHARDSON

UPPER ROOM BOOKS®
NASHVILLE

Upper Room Books website: books.upperroom.org

Upper Room®, Upper Room Books®, and design logos are trademarks owned by The Upper Room®, Nashville, Tennessee. All rights reserved.

Blessings for chapter openings are taken from Carmichael, Alexander. *Carmina Gadelica: Hymns and Incantations*, Volume I. Edinburgh: T. and A. Constable, 1900; Volume III. Edinburgh: Oliver and Boyd, 1940.

At the time of publication all website references in this book were valid. However, due to the fluid nature of the Internet some addresses may have changed or the content may not longer be relevant.

Cover: Bruce Gore | Gore Studio Inc.
Cover photo: The Quirang—Isle of Skye, Scotland, by Paul Schatzkin
        paul@cohesionarts.com © 2012. All rights reserved.
Back cover photo: Timothy Savage
Interior design: Perfect Type, Nashville, Tennessee
Opening chapter blessings taken from the following:
    Carmichael, Alexander. *Carmina Gadelica: Hymns and Incantations*, Volume I. Edinburgh: T. and A. Constable, 1900.
    Carmichael, Alexander. *Carmina Gadelica: Hymns and Incantations*, Volume III. Edinburgh: Oliver and Boyd, 1940.
    O'Donohue, John. *Anam Cara: A Book of Celtic Wisdom*. New York: HarperCollins, 1997

LIBRARY OF CONGRESS CATALOGING-IN-PUBLICATION DATA
Names: Richardson, Beth A.
Title: Christ beside me, Christ within me : Celtic blessings / Beth A. Richardson.
Description: Nashville : Upper Room Books, 2016. | Includes bibliographical references and index.
Identifiers: LCCN 2015032566| ISBN 9780835815239 (print) | ISBN 9780835815338 (mobi) | ISBN 9780835815246 (epub)
Subjects: LCSH: Prayers. | Benediction. | Celtic Church—Prayers and devotions.
Classification: LCC BV245 .R555 2016 | DDC 242/.8—dc23
LC record available at http://lccn.loc.gov/2015032566
Printed in the United States of America

TO MY CELTIC ANCESTORS—

Margaret Richardson, mother,

Tom Wilson, grandfather,

Margaret Teresa Griffin, great-grandmother,

Mary Tuohy, great-great-grandmother.

And all those who came before,
members of the community of saints.

TIMELINE

Late 1800s – John (Jack) Wilson immigrates to South Africa from England. Margaret Griffin immigrates to South Africa from Ireland. Jack and Margaret meet and marry in Kimberley, South Africa.

1899 – John and Margaret live in Kenilworth, South Africa, taking refuge in Kimberley during the Siege of Kimberley in the Second Boer War.

1905 – Jack and Tom (twins) are born in Kenilworth.

1907 – Eileen (Jack and Tom's sister) is born in Kenilworth.

1914 – Wilson family takes a trip from South Africa to England so Grandpa Jack's brother can see a doctor.

1914 (August) – England declares war on Germany. Civilian travel ceases.

1914 – Wilson family travels to Scariff, County Clare, Ireland, to visit Margaret Griffin Wilson's birthplace and family.

1915 – Wilson family waits in Liverpool for the *RMS Lusitania* with tickets to travel to the United States.

1915 (May 7) – German U-boat sinks the *Lusitania* off the coast of Ireland before it reaches port in Liverpool.

1915 – Wilson family travels to the United States on the *Philadelphia* along with survivors of the *Lusitania* disaster.

1915 – Wilson family arrives in southwest Oklahoma only to be stranded in the United States when civilian travel ceases with the onset of the US war on Germany.

1924 – Tom Wilson receives high school diploma and teacher's certificate from Cameron College in Lawton, Oklahoma.

1929 – Tom Wilson marries Hazel Davis.

1935 – Margaret Elizabeth Wilson is born.

1945 – Wilson family moves from Lawton to Norman, Oklahoma.

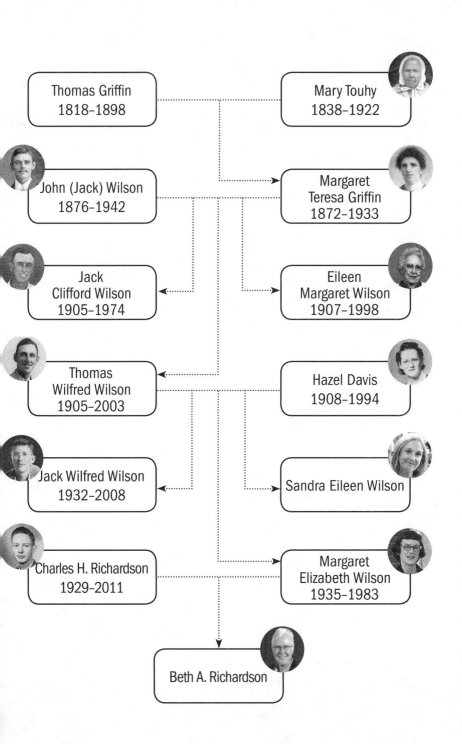

CONTENTS

5   Heart Prayers   70
Blessing the World

6   The Struggling Times   78
Facing Illness, Loss, and Grief

PREFACE

I started writing prayers in the form of blessings as I prepared to lead worship for a retreat on Celtic spirituality. This process inspired me to pull together an issue of *Alive Now* magazine on "Blessings: The Gift of Celtic Spirituality." I thought the exercise would allow me to wrap my mind and spirit around that form of prayer, a way to sink into the theme.

Often the blessings came to me early in the morning as I walked the dog. Images or words would surface in my mind and weave their way into prayers. I shared these blessings on my blog[1] and began to imagine a collection of prayers surrounding the ordinary experiences of our ordinary lives.

John O'Donohue, Irish philosopher and poet, greatly inspired me. He was born in County Clare, Ireland, the area where my Celtic family lived. In his book *Anam Cara: A Book of Celtic Wisdom*, O'Donohue writes, "The human body is clay. . . . Our clay has a memory that preceded our minds, a life of its own before it took its present form."[2] As I learned about Celtic spirituality, I began to realize *This is the way I already live.*

This way of living—observing and celebrating, blessing and being blessed by the ordinary acts and encounters of life— is who I am, is part of my clay. Perhaps it's the peat-laden clay of Scariff in County Clare, Ireland, the birthplace of my

great-grandmother, Margaret Griffin. And my way of living—
of watching bare branches of a tree against the glowing sky
of morning, of sitting in the backyard and listening to the
song of the tree frogs, of giving my life to God each morning and thanking God for the day in the evening—is a Celtic
way, full of praise, gratitude, and blessings. This way of living,
this "blessing way," was passed down to me from great-great-
grandmother, Mary Tuohy; through great-grandmother, Margaret Teresa Griffin; my grandfather, Thomas Wilfred Wilson;
and my mother, Margaret Elizabeth Richardson.

What Is a Blessing?

Celtic is the name given to the people who inhabited the far
western reaches of the Roman Empire when that empire
moved into the area in the fourth century. The linguistic ori-
gin of Celtic is the Latin *Celtae* and *Celticus*, the name given
by the Romans to those who had inhabited the islands of Ireland and Britain since prehistoric times. Today's use of *Celtic*
refers to those people whose culture and linguistic roots are
based in that ancient tradition and language, primarily Scotland, Ireland, Isle of Man, Wales, Cornwall, Brittany.

Christianity came to the Celts in the fourth century as
the Roman Empire made its way west to the far reaches of
the British Isles. Roman Christians, and Catholic missionaries
brought their religion with them, and Christianity took root
in the fertile culture of the Celts. The resulting spirituality
kept a strong Celtic personality. Celtic Christians acknowl-
edged God's presence in every aspect of living—from waking to sleeping, from birth to death, from mundane chores to
momentous celebrations. They perceived God's creation as a
holy gift. Gratitude characterized their way of being as they
affirmed the source of life and gave thanks through blessings.

Gaelic blessings (Gaelic is a language of the Celts), a prayer
form that has survived through the years, serve as the primary

inspiration for the prayers in this book. As a young adult I learned the prayer attributed to Saint Patrick, which includes these lines:

> Christ with me, Christ before me, Christ behind me,
> Christ in me, Christ beneath me, Christ above me,
> Christ on my right, Christ on my left,
> Christ when I lie down, Christ when I sit down,
> Christ in the heart of everyone who thinks of me,
> Christ in the mouth of everyone who speaks of me,
> Christ in the eye that sees me,
> Christ in the ear that hears me.

A wonderful source of Gaelic prayers is the work of Alexander Carmichael. Carmichael traveled the Scottish Highlands in the late 1800s collecting prayers, spells, and incantations from the residents. These prayers had been passed down through many generations from mother to child, from grandfather to grandson. The prayers collected by Carmichael open a window to this world of Celtic Christianity. Carmichael translated the prayers into English and published them in several volumes of *Carmina Gadelica: Hymns and Incantations*.[3]

One of my favorite prayers from this collection is "Rune before Prayer." Alexander says in the introduction,

> Old people in the Isles sing this or some other short hymn before prayer. Sometimes the hymn and the prayer are intoned in low tremulous unmeasured cadences like the moving and moaning, the soughing and the sighing, of the ever-murmuring sea on their own wild shores. They generally retire to a closet, to an outhouse, to the lee of a knoll, or to the shelter of a dell, that they may not be seen nor heard of men. I have known men and women of eighty, ninety, and a hundred years of age continue the practice of their lives in going from one to two miles to the seashore to join their voices with the voicing of

the waves and their praises with the praises of the cease-
less sea.[4]

Rune before Prayer

I am bending my knee
In the eye of the One who created me,
In the eye of the Son who purchased me,
In the eye of the Spirit who cleansed me,
    In friendship and affection.

Through your own Anointed One, O God,
Bestow upon us fullness in our need,
    Love towards God,
    The affection of God,
    The smile of God,
    The wisdom of God,
    The grace of God,
    The fear of God,
    And the will of God

To do on the world of the Three,
As angels and saints
Do in heaven;
    Each shade and light,
    Each day and night,
    Each time in kindness,
    Give us your Spirit.[5]

ACKNOWLEDGMENTS

I write this book, grateful for my Celtic heritage and the joy I receive in celebrating the ordinary moments of the day. For my brothers, Charlie and Thomas, who took the time to audio-record Grandpa Tom telling stories while sitting in the living room of his house on Rich Street in Norman, Oklahoma.

I'm grateful to Jeannie Crawford-Lee who encouraged me to find the next book that needed to be birthed and for her assistance in helping me refine the project. And for Rita Collett whose editing helped shape the book into what it has become.

The book idea galvanized when I had the opportunity to serve as worship leader for the Five-Day Academy for Spiritual Formation in Northern Alabama during the summer of 2014. In preparing for the event, which focused on Celtic spirituality, I began to write blessings. I'm grateful to Loyd Allen and Mary C. Earle who taught me much about Celtic spirituality through their lectures that week and to the leadership team who affirmed my writings.

I wrote many of these prayers as I reflected on the lives of specific people and the challenges, situations, and celebrations that they were facing. I am grateful for your friendship though I cannot name all of you who, unknowingly, significantly influenced the creation of this book.

Thank you to the staff of The Upper Room who are my spiritual family. You continue to love me, teach me, mentor me in my journey as a writer, editor, and leader.

Thank you to my aunt, Sandra Wilson Sharp, who helped me verify the details of my family history and cheered the progress of the book.

And thanks to Jenni, Jack, and Arya who fill my life with joy.

INTRODUCTION

I organized this book by chapters that contain different types of blessings. "Through the Day" includes prayers that celebrate God's presence in each moment of the day, from waking to sleeping. In "Holy Moments" I've encompassed a variety of prayers that acknowledge the richness of life's gifts—the love of pets, the ritual of morning coffee (or your favorite morning beverage), the holy gift of discovering a bird's nest. This chapter includes one of my favorite forms of blessing, "Bless to me" prayers.

The chapter "Seasons" contains prayers that mark our journeys through each year from New Year's Day through Christmas. "Passages" contains prayers for special moments in our lives such as births, marriages, and graduations. "Heart Prayers" are blessings of the world and its people.

In the chapter "The Struggling Times," I've written blessings for the many stages of hurt, illness, grief, and death that we face as we walk through life. I hope these will comfort you and those with whom you share this resource.

The book closes with an acknowledgment that "God Is In" our spirits, our relationships, our communities, our world. God is in each of us, and we are grateful.

Bless to Me Prayers

The "Bless to me" prayer is an ancient Celtic form. The prayer focuses on a tool, item, or activity in an expression of gratitude, celebrating the gift of this object or activity and the way it contributes to the pray-er's life. It is a prayer of the present moment, a specific acknowledgment of the presence of the holy, right now in this place.

Bless to me this kitchen, this truck, this walking the dog, this pillow, this washing of the dishes. Bless to me this bird song, this quiet before sunrise, these falling leaves. When I am fully present in this moment then I have taken the first step in crafting a "Bless to me" prayer. I hope you will find yourself writing these prayers in your journal or upon your heart.

My "Celtic Clay"

Nestled at the beginning of each chapter I have included a story or reflection about the life of my grandfather Tom Wilson. Grandpa shaped my life in meaningful ways and in his life my Celtic roots are grounded.

Grandpa lived an amazing life full of adventures. He was a storyteller, so I grew up knowing the stories of his life, the stories of where I came from.

Grandpa was my mother's dad. He exerted the most positive influence on my childhood. He helped me know deep down to my core that I was loved unconditionally by him and by God. He resonated with true goodness in the world.

Grandpa was born in South Africa, the son of an English father and an Irish mother who had immigrated to South Africa from their respective countries, settled in Kimberley, met, married, and had a family. John Wilson, a native of England, met and married Margaret Griffin, from Ireland. They had three children: Tom and Jack were twins. Their younger sister was Eileen. When Grandpa was ten years old, his family traveled to England so that Grandpa's twin brother, Jack, could have surgery on his arm. (Jack had broken his arm, and the doctors in South Africa were unable to fix it properly. John and Margaret intended for him to have surgery in England to save the use of his arm.) Little sister, Eileen, was eight years old. They took passage from Cape Town on the passenger ship *Balmoral Castle*. But World War I was breaking out. By the time they reached England, the country was at war, the surgeon they were to see had been drafted, and civilian travel back to South Africa was impossible.

Unable to return home, the family visited County Clare, Ireland, and spent several months with Grandpa's mother's family on the farm where she grew up. Grandpa's grandmother, Mary Touhy Griffin, lived on a farm with her son, Jim, and his wife, Mariah. The Wilsons stayed there long enough for the children to enroll in school and get to know their Irish roots a little bit. In stories that we heard from Grandpa, he noted that the schoolmaster in County Clare treated him and his siblings unkindly. He had no fondness for the British, and these three children had a British father.

Great-grandpa Wilson was trying to determine how to get the family back to their home in South Africa. He figured that the only way to get home entailed traveling through a country that was not involved in the war. Since the United States had not entered the war, the family bought passage to New York. They planned to visit relatives in Oklahoma and then return to South Africa by taking a ship from Galveston, Texas. In May of 1915, the family was waiting in Liverpool, England, with tickets to travel to the United States on the *Lusitania*. The *Lusitania* was sunk by a German U-boat off the coast of Ireland as it headed for port in Liverpool.

The family remained in England, awaiting the next ship that could take them to the United States. They embarked from Liverpool on the American liner *Philadelphia* with a number of the *Lusitania* survivors. Grandpa recalled that the fearful survivors would stay up on deck for most of the passage from England to New York.

By the time the family made it to the United States and then on to Oklahoma, the country stood on the verge of entering the war; the American lives lost in the sinking of the *Lusitania* had contributed to the call for war.

The Wilson family had traveled to southwestern Oklahoma near Lawton to visit Grandpa's aunt Mary Griffin Scott. The United States' declaration of war halted civilian travel, and the Wilsons found themselves stranded again. By the end of World War I, the family had no money to travel back home. Great-grandpa Wilson, having never farmed a day of his life, nevertheless bought a farm in southwestern Oklahoma and began to eke out a life for them in this new place.

This unusual pilgrimage from South Africa to Oklahoma changed the course of their lives, luckily for me. I was born with this rich legacy of courage and adaptability and a deep gratitude for life, whatever it presents.

Using This Book

I trust that you will use this book as a source of blessings for your life and for the lives of those you love. You also may carry the clay of the Celts or live your life as if everything is a blessing from the Creator. If this concept is new for you, I hope that this book will inspire you to open your eyes, your ears, your heart to the wonders of creation, of relationships, of adventures that surround you daily.

As I write this book, I imagine your hands thumbing through these pages, reading slowly, letting the words sink deeply into your heart.

I imagine you finding just the right blessing for a current need or marking pages to share with a friend. I envision you writing the much-needed blessing for a friend who is having a hard time or who has lost a loved one.

I picture you stopping in the middle of a walk to watch the slow progression of an ant carrying a leaf across your path. Or running outside to watch the beauty of a sunset. I imagine you, your eyes wide open, taking a photo of a spring flower, or, in the early morning, writing in your heart a blessing for a new day.

Let yourself enter this world of blessings and gratitude, of praise and pilgrimage. May you find yourself blessed by these pages whether you are new to this path or already live in a world surrounded by ordinary experiences that mark the way through an ordinary life.

May you be blessed this day. And may you walk gently into the day, ready to see blessings all around you.

1

Through the Day

Celebrating God's Presence in Each Moment

God with me lying down,
God with me rising up,
God with me in each ray of light,
Nor I a ray of joy without God,
    Nor one ray without God.

Christ with me sleeping,
Christ with me waking,
Christ with me watching.
Every day and night,
    Each day and night.

God with me protecting,
The Lord with me directing,
The Spirit with me strengthening,
For ever and for evermore.
    Ever and evermore. Amen.

—*Carmina Gadelica*, I, 5

Grandpa's Story

Grandpa was born in Kenilworth, South Africa, in 1905, the second of fraternal twin brothers. When he told the story of his birth, he said that his brother, Jack, was born first. The midwife didn't expect a second baby, so when Grandpa showed up it was a surprise. Grandpa wasn't expected to live, so he was set aside in a pile of bloody rags. But he didn't die.

I think this birth experience shaped my Grandpa. Unexpected, set aside to die, living despite the odds. Each new day, throughout his ninety-eight years, dawned as a special gift. He lived in grace, and he extended love and grace to those around him.

I was the first grandchild. Grandpa taught me to hold up one finger in the air—"You're number one," he said. But all the grandchildren were "number one" to him. When I displeased Grandma and she was scolding me, Grandpa would say to her, "Let her be. She's doing pretty good."

Grandpa, perhaps more than anyone, taught me about a God of unconditional love, a God who loves me no matter what. Through Grandpa I learned that I was loved and cherished just by being me.

When Grandpa died, someone remarked that he didn't exhibit much of a relationship with God. But I think the person was mistaken. Grandpa may not have talked about God a lot, but he walked with God each day, in every moment, through every inter-action, through every touch, and in every smile. He lived fully the gift of life that he received at his birth.

Bless Our Waking

Bless this day and all who wake.
Bless all who wake.

Bless this day and all who weep.
Bless all who weep.

Bless this day and all who fear.
Bless all who fear.

Bless this day and all who laugh.
Bless all who laugh.

Bless this day and all who hunger.
Bless all who hunger.

Bless this day and all who hope.
Bless all who hope.

Bless this day.

A Blessing of the Morning

Bless this day,
The quiet sounds of morning,
The waking of creation.

Bless this silence, Nurturer of solitude,
Feeding thirsty spirits,
Filling hearts for another day.

We breathe deeply the quiet,
The early morning sounds,
The softness of the sun.

We breathe deeply the beauty,
The songs of birds,
The dew upon the grass.

We breathe deeply the peace,
Cool wind upon skin,
Gentleness in every step.

Guide us
Gently into the day.
May we be blessings to all we meet.

A BREAKFAST BLESSING

Bless this food.
Bless this day.
Bless my steps.
Bless my words.

For clean water, for juice or milk, coffee or tea.
For food, for bread or tortillas, noodles or rice.
For those who wake with plenty, never knowing a hungry
    moment.
For those who enter their day hungry for food, craving
    comfort.

For all those who helped to make this food.
For farmers and harvesters.
For sellers and truckers.
For cooks and servers.

May all be loved this day.
May all be fed this day.
May all be blessed with your generous love.

AT THE MIDDAY

Bless this midday,
A break in my busyness,
A time to rest, renew, refresh
From the challenges of the morning.
Bless this food,
Bless this pause,
Bless this rest.

Remind me that this day,
This whole life,
Is a gift from you.

May I breathe in Spirit,
Breathe in strength,
Breathe in wisdom.

Fill this food,
Fill this pause,
Fill this rest.

I am yours.

The Evening Meal

For the seed and the soil,
The rain and the sun,
For the hands who touched, nurtured, harvested,
I give you thanks.

For the families that gather,
The ones who hunger,
The lonely people who eat by themselves,
I ask your blessing.

For this food and drink,
This plate and bowl,
These walls that protect me,
I bow in humble gratitude.

All that I have,
All that I am,
All that I will be,
Are gifts of yours,
Creator of the universe,
Creator of me.

A Blessing at Sunset

Bless, O God, this tender evening,
The trees, branches raised in praise,
The sky, soft glow darkening into dusk,
The homecoming of young and old.

Bless, O God, this sacred moment,
The quiet pause between day and night,
The birds, flying to safety in bush or brush.
The colors of the sunset—
Orange to red to purple to black—
Creeping across the sky.

Bless, O God, this night to come.
The safety of shelter, the supper to nourish.
Hearts of joy or souls bent in sorrow.
Renewing rest and hope for one more day.

Bless, O God. Bless.

NIGHT

Bless this night.
The light gives way to the darkness,
And another day is done.

Bless those I have met this day
And those whose faces come to my mind.

Bless the smiles, words, and thoughts
That touched your creatures, large and small.

Forgive, O God, the sins of your servant this day:
The unkind word or thought,
The deed of which I am ashamed.
Forgive me, that I may find rest in you.

Bless this house, this pillow, this bed.
May I lie down in your peace and love,
And awake again to be your hands and heart in the world.
I am yours, God of love.
Bless this night.

2

Holy Moments

Celebrating the Gifts of Life

Bless to me, O God,
   Each thing my eye sees;
Bless to me, O God,
   Each sound my ear hears;
Bless to me, O God,
   Each odor that goes to my nostrils;
Bless to me, O God,
   Each taste that goes to my lips;
   Each note that goes to my song,
   Each ray that guides my way,
   Each thing that I pursue,
   Each lure that tempts my will,
   The zeal that seeks my living soul,
The Three that seek my heart,
   The zeal that seeks my living soul,
The Three that seek my heart.

—*Carmina Gadelica*, III, 33

Grandpa's Story

*Among the few heirlooms from Grandpa's family was a worn and
battered bank book from the Bank of Ulster. The first page shows
a deposit on November 20, 1914, of 350 pounds to the account
of Mrs. Margaret Wilson, Scariff, County Clare. Grandpa's mom
would have opened the account during the several months that
the family visited the Griffin home place in Ireland.*

*After the family left Ireland for the United States, the bank
book reflected the daily records of life on the farm. Their currency
changed from shillings and pounds to eggs, cream, and furs. The
farm records in the bank book span from 1915 to 1922. The family kept records for hens, fryers, chicks, roosters, eggs, cows, calves,
cream, butter, turkeys, pigs, furs, and work done. In various persons' handwriting, in ink and pencil, in the cultured handwriting of Great-grandma Margaret and the quick scrawl of, perhaps,
Grandpa Tom, the monthly records reveal a life scraped out of the
red clay of Oklahoma. Below is a sampling:*

Sale of eggs
February 2 — 4 dozen, $1.80
February 7 — 13 dozen, $5.20
February 13 — 9 dozen, $2.70

Sale of cream
February 15 — $3.01
February 20 — $3.44

Milk cows
Blossom
Maude
Jenny
Violet

Peggy
Bessie

Calving list
Peggie "took" August 16. Due May 16.
Dane "took" December 3. Due September 3.

Work done
21 November 1919 — Worked 5 hours on Bottom Road.

Purchases
Ford Runabout bought March 10, 1922. Paid $415.50 without license and gas.

Great-grandma Margaret died of a heart attack in 1933 at the age of sixty-one. Born in the greenest of green in Ireland, she immigrated to the veld of Africa. She ended up raising chickens on the dry, hard, red clay of Oklahoma. Grandpa Tom said that her heart was broken; she never got over the loss of her homes.

But something compelled Margaret to keep writing in that little bank book turned farm journal. And I hope that, though the treeless lands of southwest Oklahoma differed greatly from the lush greenness of Ireland, perhaps she found God's grace and beauty in the daily tasks of life: gathering eggs and milking cows, witnessing glorious sunsets and the beauty of the sky, watching her children grow in love.

WALKING THE DOG

Bless to me this walking of the dog.
Early in morning, late at night,
We walk to the park and back.

Bless to me the silence we share.
Me watching, him sniffing,
Noticing the changes of each day, each season.

Bless to me my faithful companion.
In him I see the world
Through different eyes and ears and nose.

Bless to me this quiet time.
Our ritual, a time of prayer,
Of peace, of love.

Bless to me this walking of the dog.

A Blessing of the Coffee

Bless this cup,
Smooth and warm,
Held in cold hands,
    In cold hands.

Bless this drink,
Dark and strong,
Sipped slowly in the quiet,
    In the quiet.

Bless the beans
And those who picked them.
All who washed and roasted,
    Washed and roasted.

Bless the workers
And their families,
Their children and their homes,
    And their homes.

Bless this day
And all who wake.
Give them comfort, strength, and plenty,
    Strength and plenty.

Bless this coffee,
Warm and sweet.
Nourishing, comforting taste of love,
    Taste of love.

THIS SABBATH DAY

Bless to me this new day.
The sounds and sights
And smells and tastes.
The cool breeze on my cheek
And the warm sun on my head.

Bless to me this sabbath time.
Space to rest, to play,
To feel the fullness of this life.

Bless to me this gift of plenty.
Of food and shelter,
Of peace and safety,
Of freedom from worry
And abundance to share.

Bless to me this space
To hold in love all those
Who struggle in life,
Who sit in sorrow,
Who walk and wait and run in fear.

Bless the earth
And all its creatures.
Bless to me this new day.

A Blessing of a Bird Nest

So fragile, this nest,
Sitting on the electrical box,
Barely sheltered from the wind and the rain.

So fragile, these eggs,
Life growing within,
Nurtured by the warmth
Of a mother's tiny body.

Life begins,
Life grows,
Life comes forth
From miraculous beginnings.

Shelter these lives,
Great God of creation,
Source of all that has been,
All that is,
And all that is to come.

Thank you, Creator,
For eyes to see
Intricate nests,
Tiny birds,
Speckled eggs.

Delight of your creation.

A Blessing of a Summer Day

Bless this day,
All plants and creatures,
All people near and far.

Bless the flowers
That sing praises with their beauty,
The grass
That cushions my step.

Bless those who stand
With loved ones who are sick,
With friends or family who are lost.
Bring healing, bring wholeness.

Bless the world,
Its war-torn places,
Its broken villages,
Its frightened children.

Bless our bodies,
Our hearts,
Our hands,
That we may be blessings
To all we meet.

SITTING WITH AN AGING PET

You still chase bunnies in your sleep.
Tracking, barking, leaping,
Master of the backyard.

You still jump in the air when it's time to eat,
Letting me know that you know
When supper time is here.

But then I see you dodge a shadow,
Unable to see clearly with cloudy eyes.
And I have to touch you when I enter the room
To let you know I am here.

I know that someday
Your windmill tail will stop spinning;
Your courageous, loyal heart will cease to beat.

I sit with you in love and sadness and gratitude.
I hope that I have blessed you
With just a fraction of the blessing
You have given me.
And I am grateful for your sweetness, your faithfulness.

You still chase bunnies in your sleep.

SOWING SEED

God of the earth,
Creator of the universe,
Bless this seed that I plant this day.

For the seed, for the soil,
For the rain, for the sun,
For the miracle of life,
I humbly give you thanks.

For the plant that grows from the seed,
For the life that comes from death,
I humbly give you thanks.

Let me be a caregiver,
Servant of you,
Servant of your creation.

Bless this seed that I plant this day.

WASHING THE DISHES

Bless to me these dishes,
The plates, the glasses, the silverware,
The pots and pans that held the meal.

Bless to me this clean, warm water and soap,
This dishwasher,
These hands I use to scrub and rinse.

Bless to me this quiet time,
This family preparing for bed,
Tired bodies yearning for rest.

Bless to me this kitchen, clean,
This family, cared for,
This night, descending.

Bless to me this life of love.

3

❧

Seasons

Journeying through a Year

God, bless to me the new day,
Never vouchsafed to me before:
It is to bless your own presence
You have given me this time, O God.

Bless to me my eye.
May my eye bless all it sees;
I will bless my neighbor,
May my neighbor bless me.

God, give me a clean heart,
Let me not from sight of your eye;
Bless to me my children and my spouse,
And bless to me my means and my possessions.

—*Carmina Gadelica,* I, 159

Grandpa's Story

After World War II, Grandpa and Grandma moved from the farm near Lawton, Oklahoma, to the city of Norman. Grandpa got a job at the University of Oklahoma as a carpenter and took up gardening in the backyard of their home. When visitors came to the house, they would first receive a tour of the garden. Grandpa fed himself and Grandma, the neighbors, the extended family, and still had vegetables left over to sell at the farmers' market at McFarlin Methodist Church on Sunday morning.

The garden encompassed the entire backyard and had three plantings of crops each year. Potatoes went into the ground in February. After the potato harvest, then Grandpa planted field peas. In that same spot in the fall, rows of turnips grew. Elsewhere in the garden he planted onions, carrots, okra, corn, squash, green beans, tomatoes, and anything else he desired.

When the tree roots from across the alley started to invade, Grandpa "planted" corrugated metal six feet into the ground all around the garden's footprint.

Grandpa composted the leaves and grass clippings from the entire neighborhood. He picked up the leftover manure from the county fair and added it to the compost pile. Sometimes, the compost pile was taller than he was and he hiked up a path to the top of the pile to dump out the kitchen scraps.

When I finally had a garden of my own, I planted a few vegetables. But mostly I planted flowers. I showed Grandpa photographs of the flowers I had grown. He said, "They're pretty, but you can't eat them."

One family story that Grandpa told took place before his birth. When Great-grandpa and Great-grandma Wilson lived in South Africa, they were caught up in the Siege of Kimberley, which took place in the winter of 1899 during the Boer war. The Boers were fighting the British and besieged Kimberley for 124 days. The Boers, the descendants of the Dutch settlers of South Africa, surrounded the primarily British town of Kimberley. Since the Wilsons were British, they went into Kimberley to be protected from the Boers. As the siege continued, those within the town of Kimberley received rations of meat from the town leaders. One week the meat ration was the kidney of a horse, the story goes; Great-grandma couldn't bear to eat it. Great-grandpa Wilson started thinking of the garden he had left at his home in Kenilworth. One night, he took a gunny sack and crossed enemy lines to harvest the root vegetables that were wintering in the garden. Grandpa Tom said that thorns had overtaken the garden, and no one realized there was food under all the weeds.

Grandpa never took credit for the abundance of his backyard garden. He said that all he did was plant the seeds. God created the soil, sent the sun and the rain that nurtured the seeds, and made the plants grow. Mom cross-stitched this prayer for him, "Who plants a seed beneath the sod and waits to see believes in God."

A Blessing for the New Year

God, your hope, your joy
Be upon this new year.

God, your love, your wisdom
Fill my heart, my mind, my life.

God, your strength, your comfort
Enter every heart.

God, your guidance, your peace
Be upon every heart, every community, every nation.

On the Eve of Ash Wednesday

On the eve of Ash Wednesday,
Of spring and new life,
Of the Lenten journey.

I am overwhelmed with too much.
Too many tasks, responsibilities, voices,
Too many distractions and demands.

Take this frozen and tired soul, loving God.
Nurture within me sustaining life.
Coax from me only that which is needed.

Let me shed the darkness
That I might reach toward your light.
Let me empty cluttered spaces
That there may be a home for you.

Melt me, mold me, fill me, use me
On this eve of Ash Wednesday.

Welcome, Spring

Long nights and cold days,
Fallow fields and dormant trees,
A journey of the inner world.

I open my eyes and see light.
Warmth breaking through,
Promise of new life
Coming out of death.
Resurrection.

Welcome, beauty.
Welcome, buds.
Welcome, newness.
Inside and all around me.

You, God, source of hope,
Source of healing,
Source of life.
Welcome, welcome.
Make your home in me.

GOOD FRIDAY

Day of darkness, death, despair,
Abandoned by hope.

Hard reality sets in,
Leaving us empty.

How can we accept,
How can we believe
That life could return
From this valley of death?

God of love and mercy, save us.
We are lost and alone,
Yearning for your comfort.

Come quickly,
Lord of hope,
Bringer of life,
Come.

EASTER

Bless this day
When light returns,
Love astounds,
Life prevails.

Bless the grieving,
The lonely,
The hungry.
Hope is reborn.

Bless the young ones
And the old.
Bless the enemies
And those despised.

Bless this world,
Gripped by violence.
Peace returns.

God makes a way
Where there was no way.
Christ has risen.
Alleluia.

MEMORIAL DAY

Leave flowers at grave sites,
On street corners, and at memorials.
Leave candles and letters,
Bundles of sage
or crosses made of twigs.

Let all know
That they are not forgotten,
That their lives,
No matter how short or long,
Made a difference.
That their names,
Famous or unknown,
Will never die.

Their presence in this world
Changed it, touched it,
Marked it in a unique way.

Each one.
Every one.
Remembered.

In love,
In respect,
In gratitude.

Harvest

With grateful thanks
We receive the bounty of this earth.

Giver of plenty,
You are the source of
Plants and meat,
Milk and herbs,
Clean water and safe homes.

Bless this harvest,
Its beautiful colors.
Bless this bounty,
Its nourishing substance.

Bless the livestock
And those who keep them.
Bless the farmers, the workers,
The gleaners, far and near.

Bless the hungry,
Those who have no homes,
Those displaced by drought or violence.
Give succor to the people in their need.

Bless this world and all its creatures.
All that we are,
All that we have,
Are gifts of your creation.

ALL SAINTS DAY

For all the saints . . .
Who birthed and nurtured,
Mothers and fathers,
Grandfathers and grandmothers,
Aunts, uncles, cousins, friends,
We are grateful. Alleluia, alleluia!

For all the saints . . .
Who loved and cherished,
Husbands, wives, partners,
Friends and lovers,
We are grateful. Alleluia, alleluia!

For all the saints . . .
Who died too soon,
Whose absence pains us still.
We remember with tears,
Aches in our hearts,
And yet, we are grateful. Alleluia, alleluia!

For all the saints . . .
Who taught and mentored,
Teachers and spiritual directors,
Older friends and younger prophets,
Guiding us, inspiring us,
We are grateful. Alleluia, alleluia!

For all the saints . . .
Who watch over us,
Pray for us,
Sit with us,
Guide us,
We are grateful.
Alleluia, alleluia, alleluia!

A Blessing for the Long Nights

God's peace to you in the twilight,
in the long winter night.

God's comfort to you in the sadness,
in the mournful places of your soul.

God's courage to you in your weakness,
facing turmoil, facing trial.

God's love to you in your pain,
in the sadness of the small one who weeps inside of you.

God's presence to you in your loneliness,
in the dark, empty corners of your heart.

God's peace, God's comfort, God's love,
God's blessing be yours.

A Blessing of the Light

When the days are dreary and the light is dim,
When it seems that the world is hopeless,
Full of illness, violence, and death,
Bless the tender signs of hope we see
In the newborn child, in the generosity of the stranger.

When the night is long and tragedy reigns,
When acts of hate drown out voices of justice,
Children dying, mothers crying,
Bless the tenacious love to which we cling,
Love that hangs on, though we would sink into despair.

When all around us is sadness and grief,
When each new day brings news of illness,
Stories of disease, announcements of death,
Bless the promise of a light that shines through darkness,
Light of a star, light of a smile, light of a babe.

Bless the tears,
Bless the grief,
Bless the despair,
Bless the dying.

Bless the hope,
Bless the love,
Bless the life,
Bless the light.

Come, Emmanuel, God with us,
And bring us light.

CHRISTMAS

Bless the shepherds,
Bless the angels,
Bless the donkey, the sheep, the cow
Who share their home with a newborn babe.

Bless Joseph, wise protector.
Bless Mary, gentle mother of God.
Bless the night and the star,
The quiet gift of hope freely given.

Bless the birth,
Bless the babe,
Bless the hoped-for peace on earth
And goodwill for all.

Bless this world,
Bless this community,
Bless those loved and those who are lonely,
The joyous and the grieving ones.

Bless this house,
Bless this family,
Bless these hearts joined together
Across the table, across the miles.

Bless this night,
Bless this day,
Bless this holy time,
Gentle gift of love.

4

Passages

Special Moments

In name of God,
In name of Jesus,
In name of Spirit,
The perfect Three of power.

The little drop of the Creator
On your little forehead, beloved one.

The little drop of the Son
On your little forehead, beloved one.

The little drop of the Spirit
On your little forehead, beloved one.

To aid you, to guard you,
To shield you, to surround you.

—*Carmina Gadelica*, III, 17

Grandpa's Story

Spending time with Grandpa and Grandma at their house in Norman, Oklahoma, provided special childhood memories. In contrast to the upheaval of his childhood, Grandpa's later life was one of stability. Once he and Grandma moved off the farm, they moved to the city and lived in the same house for the rest of their lives. Grandpa's life was filled with rituals, and when I visited their home, I entered a world of sacredness, an honoring of life.

When guests arrived, they received a tour of the garden to see what was growing, to hear what had been harvested, to learn what was coming next. I would stand with Grandpa at the edge of the garden and admired the miracle of abundance that God had given.

Grandpa awakened early to do chores. He began the day by reading his Upper Room devotional and Bible. Daily he put a spoonful of vinegar, honey, and wheat germ oil in a cup of hot water and drank the mixture. (He believed this concoction was a key to health but could never persuade me to try it.) I remember his bringing a glass of orange juice to me in bed, making me feel special.

Grandpa watched the morning news and weather and drove his truck to work at the carpenter's shop at the university. He came home for lunch each day—Grandma served his lunch on a TV tray in the living room while he watched the noon news. (After he retired, they both watched Grandma's soap opera.)

The family spent summer evenings sitting in the backyard watching the purple martins swooping across the sky, eating mosquitoes. Grandpa kept track of how many plants he planted, how many bushels of produce he harvested, how much rain had fallen. He and Grandma stored root vegetables and canned vegetables in the cellar he dug out of the red clay under the garage. (The cellar also served as a tornado shelter.)

Whenever I visited, I always accompanied Grandpa to the carpenter shop for an afternoon. I delighted in sweeping up the sawdust with a big broom or hammering tacks into a piece of wood with a tack hammer. I marveled at the number of keys hanging in the room where keys were cut. We went to see the fire engine in the firehouse and got a candy bar out of the candy machine.

Game day during football season involved a different ritual. Grandpa dressed in his red blazer and red tie and made his way to the stadium to watch the game. For over fifty years, he rode the bus to Dallas on a Saturday in October to watch the Oklahoma-Texas football game. If his team lost, he would say, "They'll do better next time."

At Thanksgiving or Christmas dinner, family gathered around a table laden with food. Grandpa's prayer was this, "Bless us, O Lord, and these thy gifts which we are about to receive from thy bounty." Usually a roasted turkey graced the table and, at some point near the end of the meal, Grandpa would say, "I believe that was the best turkey we ever had."

Each grandchild received a bag of candy at Christmastime. And Grandpa always slipped us money at some point in our visit. When I began to drive to Grandpa's house, I would inevitably find my car washed and filled up with gas for my return trip.

Each visitor left the house with a bag or box of vegetables. This presented some challenges when the visitor had flown to Oklahoma; but more than once, a box of produce was checked as baggage and arrived in Tennessee without damage.

These rituals, this stability, created a feeling of safety and comfort for me when I visited Grandpa and Grandma. I breathed in the rituals of each day, of the seasons of the year, of generous love, of honoring the presence of the holy in the ordinary events of life.

A CHILD IS COMING

Bless you.
And bless this one who grows within you,
This miracle of creation.

Knit together with dust
From a thousand stars,
With clay from faraway places,
With cells descended from the dawn of life,
Child of yours, child of creation.

Walk slowly through these days,
Savoring this holy time.
Live gently in this space
Of growth and new life
Inside you, beside you, around you.

Thanks be to the One who created all,
Who created you,
Who created the life you nurture.

You are beloved.
You are chosen.
You are blessed.

A Blessing for a New Baby

Welcome to the world, little one.
We have been waiting for you
With hope and prayers.
And now you are here.

You are a miracle child,
Knit together in your mother's womb.
Formed in the image of Creation—
Of stars and planets,
Of trees and flowers,
Of humans and creatures,
Of the Creator who gave you life.

Bless, child,
Your fingers and toes,
Your feet and legs,
Your hands and arms,
Your ears and nose and mouth.
All the parts of you born in love.

Bless, child,
Your family today,
Your family to come.
Every day of your life,
May you know you are loved.

Beloved child of your parents,
Beloved child of your family,
Beloved child of God.
Welcome.

First Day of School

Bless this day of new beginnings.
Bless this lunch box, this backpack,
These new supplies: pencils or crayons, books or
     computer.

Bless the school and all who work there.
Principals, cafeteria workers,
Those who teach and those who clean.

Bless this learner, beloved of God.
Bless head and heart, hands and feet.
Prepare him for the work of learning.
Protect her as she walks the way to knowledge.

Creator, Christ, and Holy Spirit,
Be in the teaching and in the learning,
Be in the traveling and in the friending.
Be in this one you have created
As this journey begins.

Birthday

The angels sang the day you were born.
"Welcome to the world, little one!
We can't wait to see who you will become."

The heavens rejoiced
To see you make your way in life.
You are loved and beloved, a child of God.

We celebrate the You you have become.
Created and creative,
Friend of all you meet.

Bless this day,
The day you were born.
Stars and mountains, children and old ones
Rejoice in you.

AFTER THE DEATH OF A PET

You forget and put out her food.
You look at his favorite spot to nap.
You glance behind you, thinking she is still there.
And the grief bubbles up within you.

You remember the day he first came into your life,
The way your hearts bonded
Through snuggles, through play, through quiet time
    together.
Her death has left a hole in your heart
That can never, ever be filled by another being.

The sadness, the sorrow, the tears . . .
May these hurts be touched by whispers of love,
Tempered by shadows of gratitude,
Soothed by memories of joy.

Know that he will not be forgotten.
She has a place forever,
In the pattern of your life,
In the fabric of your heart.

GRADUATION

Bless this day
And bless this moment,
A celebration of your work,
Your dedication, your learning.

Bless the past
And bless the future,
All those who mentored,
Taught, and guided you.

Bless this threshold
And bless your journey.
Wise ones walk with you,
Whisper to you, protect you.

Bless this day
And bless this moment,
Your ending, your beginning,
Your special day.

FOR A HOME

Bless this house, its windows, its rooms.
May those who live here
Know happiness and safety.

Bless this house, its roof, its doors.
May all who enter here
Be welcomed with generous hospitality.

Bless this house, its hearth, its heart.
May light and love
Live in this place.

MARRIAGE

You pause on the threshold of a new life,
Looking back on all that has been,
Remembering the threads that, when woven together,
Make you who you are.

You are unique, beloved of God, a gift of love.
And now you face the future,
Together in hope, in love, in life.

The fabric of your separateness has begun to join,
Stitched together in a new pattern:
Your lives, stitched together,
Sacred patterns of trust, of hope, of love.

God's spirit surrounds you.
God's blanket of strength enfolds you.
God's love fills you.

Bless this day.
Bless this union of hearts and lives.
You are beloved of God who
Blesses your steps.

Each moment, each day,
Each sorrow, each joy,
Each new day
Of your new life.

A LEAVING

For a time
This has been your home.
But today you are leaving
And traveling to a new place, a new home.

For each day, each memory,
Each joyful moment or difficult learning,
We offer gratitude and thanks.

For your future,
A canvas of promise ready for your palette,
We offer blessings and good wishes.

May you walk in hope, in peace, in happiness.
May the Spirit guide you and protect you
All the days of your life.

Bless your journey,
Bless your paths,
Bless your life.

5

Heart Prayers

Blessing the World

Peace between neighbors,
Peace between kindred,
Peace between lovers,
    In the love of the Source of life.

Peace between person and person,
Peace between wife and husband,
Peace between woman and children,
    The peace of Christ above all peace.

Bless, O Christ, my face,
    Let my face bless every thing;
Bless, O Christ, my eye,
    Let my eye bless all it sees.

                    —*Carmina Gadelica*, III, 267

Grandpa's Story

Grandpa was a storyteller. I loved to sit with him in the living room and listen to him tell the stories of his life—from his birth to his family's accidental immigration to Oklahoma; from his school days to his family's struggles in surviving the Great Depression. He told the stories of his life and his family's life— stories that told me who I am.

Grandpa's father was a carpenter and taught both his sons the carpentry trade. One of the apprenticeship tests involved recreating a handsaw from scratch. A handsaw's teeth were filed off so that the edge was a straight line. The apprentice carpenter would use a file to cut new saw teeth into the edge of the saw and then set the teeth correctly (one tooth set to the left and the next to the right). At the end of the test, the apprentice would turn the saw on an angle with the teeth facing up and slide a finishing nail down the length of the saw through the middle of the teeth. If the nail got stuck any place along the way, the apprentice failed the test.

After the family settled in Oklahoma, Grandpa and his siblings attended the local public schools. The local children teased them because of their different clothes and speech. At the appropriate age, Grandpa and his brother, Jack, were sent to Cameron College to receive an education. Great-grandpa and Great-grandma wanted their children to have a better life than they had had.

Grandpa graduated near the top of his class and intended to become a teacher. He got letters of recommendation and started applying for teaching jobs in the area. Despite numerous openings for teachers, no one would hire him. After looking for and not finding a job across a wide area, Grandpa visited a friend of his who was the superintendent of a school. Grandpa told his friend about applying everywhere and not getting a job. He asked if his friend knew the reason.

His friend said, "Tom, I'm going to show you a letter, but I'll deny it if you tell anyone that you saw it here." It was a letter from the local organization of the Ku Klux Klan to the school superintendent. The letter stated that Tom Wilson was not to be given a teaching job because he was foreign born and Catholic.

Grandpa said he wanted to see this "Klu" Klux Klan, so he got on his mule one night and rode over to one of their meetings. He stated that it was the most ridiculous thing he had ever seen—grown men acting that way.

Grandpa never got a teaching job and spent the rest of his life as a carpenter. I never heard him complain about not being a teacher. He lived a life of acceptance, of gratitude for what he had rather than regret for what he did not have.

May You Know Love

Today, may you know love.
May you know happiness.
May you know peace.

Today, may you be open.
May you be safe.
May you be blessed.

Today, may you feel uplifted.
May you feel serene.
May you feel joy.

A thousand, thousand prayers,
A thousand, thousand blessings,
On you, and you, and you.

You Walk beside Us

We are lonely,
We are aching,
We are grieving;
You walk beside us.

We are hurting,
We are searching,
We are afraid;
You walk beside us.

We are hungry,
We are homeless,
We are destitute;
You walk beside us.

We are happy,
We are contented,
We are grateful;
You walk beside us.

On all paths,
Through all days,
For all souls,
You walk beside us.

Too Much

Some days
It seems like
Too much to bear.

Too much sickness,
Too much dying,
Too many stories of terror and sadness.

How can I bear it?
These people I love
Are crazy with grief and fear.
This world I love
Has lost all sense and reason.

I watch, I weep, I wait.
I wait for you to show up
With your healing,
Your comfort,
Your wisdom.

Come quickly.
Please,
Be present.

BEAUTY BEFORE YOU

Beauty before you.
Beauty behind you.
Beauty within you.

Beauty feed you.
Beauty refresh you.
Beauty nourish you.

Beauty in your hands.
Beauty in your presence.
Beauty in your heart.

Open your eyes,
Your senses,
Your soul
To beauty.

THE HURTING PLACES

There is a world of hurt around me today,
And my heart fills with pain.
Sometimes I hear myself saying,
"All I can do is pray."

And then I remember that praying
Is no small thing.
Sometimes it is the only thing,
The one true thing for this hurting world.

Healing God, send your wholeness,
Loving Christ, your strength,
Holy Spirit, your comforting presence,
To all who hurt,
To all who struggle,
To all who mourn. Amen.

6

The Struggling Times

Facing Illness, Loss, and Grief

Be this soul on your arm, O Christ,
You, Ruler of the City of Heaven.
 Amen.

Since you, O Christ, it was who bought this soul,
Be its peace on your own keeping.
 Amen.

And may the strong Michael, high king of the
 angels,
Be preparing the path before this soul, O God.
 Amen.

O! the strong Michael in peace with you, soul,
And preparing for you the way to the reign of the
 Son of God.
 Amen.

—*Carmina Gadelica*, I, 117

Grandpa's Story

Grandpa Tom married Grandma Hazel on October 26, 1929. The stock market crashed on October 29. Grandpa always said that the crash didn't matter much to them—they had spent all their money getting married three days before. But it did mean that times were hard as they began their marriage. They lived with Grandpa's dad, raised chickens, and farmed as they could in the midst of the Depression and the Dust Bowl. Grandpa traveled to whatever work he could find, serving as a carpenter and laborer on construction crews. In 1939 he worked 23 weeks and made seven hundred dollars.

Grandpa's life was filled with hard times: from his family's immigration to America to his poverty in Oklahoma to the dashed dreams of his vocation because of discrimination. He lived a life of love and grace, remaining positive in the face of disappointment. After Grandma died, he continued to live at home. In his nineties, he took in his younger sister, Eileen, when she could no longer live alone, and they shared his house until she passed away. He lived until the age of ninety-eight and died at home.

Grandpa trusted in God's presence in the midst of struggles. He accepted the hardships of life without sinking into despair. When a tornado blew away the chicken house, he rebuilt it. When the KKK made sure he didn't get a teaching job, he worked the carpenter trade he had learned from his father. When Grandma died of a heart attack, he kept living: planting, harvesting, greeting at church, attending football games, telling stories, loving his family.

Grandpa lived fully, with love and grace, until he died. That is the hope I have for my life: that I will face the challenges that come my way and live fully, trusting God in love and in grace.

FOR ONE WHO IS HURTING

God, your peace,
Your comfort,
Your healing presence.

Send them into
The places of deep sadness,
The wounds,
The disappointments,
The tears and aching hearts.

Touch the tear-lined cheeks
With your kiss of peace.

Hold your child close,
Child full of sorrow.
Hold your child close,
Child all alone.

Bring comfort and healing,
Balm for broken hearts,
Freedom from fear,
And courage to face forward.

You are the Miracle Worker,
The Great Healer,
The Mender of the Breach.

Come, now,
Come, quickly,
Come.

Facing Illness

We ask your blessing, healing God,
For your beloved child.

Guide the hands, the hearts, the wisdom
Of doctors and nurses.

Wrap family, friends, and loved ones
With compassion and courage.

Shelter this loved one
With strength and comfort.

Surround this child with your love.
Hold this beloved in your peace.

You are the Creator,
The Healer,
The Comforter.
The Source of love.

Choosing a Path

We have come
To a place of decision
That may change
The course of a life.

Your love, God of Creation,
Be in our hearts.

Your courage, God of Strength,
Be in our spirits.

Your guidance, God of Wisdom,
Be in our considerations.

Bless our struggling.
Bless our discernment.
Bless our paths.

Guide our thoughts.
Guide our words.
Guide our steps.

A Holy Pilgrimage

You walk a holy journey
You have never walked before,
Full of tears and gratitude,
Gentle conversations,
Silences filled with love.

No one knows the way,
But you meet each twist and turn
With discernment and courage,
Hope and faith.

You walk this pilgrimage,
In many ways, by yourself—
But you are never truly alone.

Others walk before you, behind you, beside you,
Surrounding you with love,
Wrapping you in hope,
Touching your spirits in peace.

You are loved,
You are held,
You are God's.

You Sit by the Bedside

You sit by the bedside
Holding a hand, holding the space
For one who is entering the final journey.

You sit by the bedside on a holy pilgrimage,
Never having gone there yourself,
Trusting that your presence is enough.

You sit by the bedside of one who is silent,
Of one who is crying,
Of one who is drifting away.

You enter the thin space, the holy place,
Hand holding hand,
Spirit touching spirit.

You sit by the bedside,
Praying and singing,
A witness of love and courage.

Go gently, dear friend.
The saints travel with you.
Bless this time, this journey, this transition.

You sit by the bedside.
God in you and God in the beloved one.
Christ in sorrow and Christ in freedom.
Spirit holding all.

THE SHADOWLANDS

When the one you love
Is no longer there,
Hidden in the shadowlands
Between life and death.
When all you can do is hold a hand,
Stroke a cheek.

When eyes well up
At the smallest kindness
Or tears pour down your cheeks
Like they will never stop.

When valiant caregivers
Have done all they can
And can do no more.

When there are no words,
When there is no comfort,
When you are lost
In the shock and the grief.

You are not alone.
You are surrounded with love
Of family,
Of friends,
Of those who have gone before.

You both are held in light,
Surrounded by love.
Do not fear for you are flanked by angels.
You . . . are beloved of the Holy One.

A Blessing of the Grief

Heaven weeps with you. . . .
Your loved one has died,
Joined the company of the saints.
Sitting with the ancestors,
Singing with angels,
Watching over you in love.

And none of those images,
None of these promises,
Can take away the exquisite grief
That leaks out of your eyes,
That has taken up residence in your heart.

Bless the grief that breathes in you.
Bless the sorrow that leaves you lost.
Bless the emptiness that can never be filled.
The Holy One is in each breath, each tear,
    each empty corner of your being.

Bless the love that penetrates your numbness.
Bless the heart that connects you forever
    with the one you have lost.
Bless the Holy One who sits with you,
    breathes with you, cries with you.

You are beloved and loved.
You are not alone.

A BLESSING OF THE EMPTY SPACE

You sit in the empty place that is left,
After the death, the arrangements, the service,
The cards and calls and e-mails,
The departure of family,
The thank-yous and acknowledgments.

Left with the emptiness,
The space that can never be filled
In quite the same way.

You see a shadow, hear a sound,
Taste a food they used to love,
Start to tell them something about your day,
Smell a blanket or sweater,
And your eyes and heart fill with tears.

The first week, the first month, the first birthday,
The first holiday, the first anniversary,
These bring you to the place of remembering,
The place of exquisite, lonely sorrow.

Bless you and your memories.
Bless the tender heart that beats within you.
Bless the empty space that can never be filled.

The shadows, the smells, the tastes, the thoughts,
Transform their pain into blessings,
Signs that though you live in that desperately empty
    place,
Your loved ones accompany you,
Laugh in the shelter of your heart.

The empty place
That can never be filled
In quite the same way
Is filled
With love.

Some Days Are Very Hard

Some days are very hard.
And on those days
May you know that you are loved,
You are held,
You are not alone.

Some days are very hard.
And on those days
May you remember that
Hope and healing surround you.

And if you cannot remember,
If you cannot trust,
If you cannot feel the Presence,
We will remember and trust
And feel and believe
On your behalf.

Some days are very hard.
And on those days
May light and love
Soothe your heart,
Calm your mind,
Heal your spirit,
Surround you in peace.

7

～ల~

God Is In

Celebrating Presence

God to enfold me,
   God to surround me,
God in my speaking,
   God in my thinking.

God in my sleeping,
   God in my waking,
God in my watching,
   God in my hoping.

God in my life,
   God in my lips,
God in my soul,
   God in my heart.

God in my sufficing,
   God in my slumber,
God in my ever-living soul,
   God in my eternity.

                    —*Carmina Gadelica*, III, 53

Grandpa's Story

God resides in every part of life. And God was in every part of Grandpa's life.

God was in his ancestors, in their simple lives in the hamlets, farms, and cities of Ireland and England. God was in their births and deaths, their loving and their grieving. God was in their leavings and their coming homes.

God was in the journey of Margaret Griffin from Ireland to South Africa, in the journey of John Wilson from England to South Africa. In their meeting and their courting. In their marriage and in their love. In their life as a family far from the soil of their homes.

God was in the strange journey of the Wilson family from South Africa to England to Ireland to the United States. God was in the red-clay soil of Oklahoma, in the cotton seeds, in the flat land and the scouring wind, in the breathtaking sky at sunset and the brilliant stars of night.

God was in each moment of Grandpa's life, from his precarious birth in South Africa to his peaceful death in his bed at home in Oklahoma. God was in his waking and in his sleeping. God was in his planting and his harvesting. God was in his strong hands as they held hammer and saw, plumb line and chisel. God was in his love of family, friend, and stranger, his storytelling and his carpentry. God was in his loyalty to his church home, his extravagant gifts of produce, and his role as a steward of the earth.

God is in the legacy of generosity and gentleness passed on to his children, grandchildren, great-grandchildren, and great-great-grandchildren. God is in the values and memories, the stories that live in my heart. God is in all of life. All of me. All of us.

THIS DAY

Dawn of Life,
Dawn of Love,
We greet you.

Bless us this day,
And bless all we meet:
The grieving friend,
The laughing child,
The stranger on the corner.

Fill our hearts with your light
And let that light shine through us,
Bringing friendship and hope,
Peace and presence.

We are yours.

CHRIST BEFORE US

Christ before us.
Christ behind us.
Christ beside us.
Christ within us.
O Christ, be in this place.

Seasons

As the seasons change,
We turn to you, God of creation,
Our source, our wisdom, our comfort.

Be our anchor in the midst of turmoil.
Our healing spirit in times of brokenness.
Our blessing in the emptiness.
We are yours. Amen.

You, O God

You, O God!
You paint the sky with our prayers.

You, O Great Gardener!
You coax forth delicate buds and blooms.

You, O Mighty One!
You bend your ear to our laments, our praises.

You, O Gentle Spirit!
You delight in creatures great and small.

Shelter us with your love.
Enliven us with your passion.
Kiss us with your peace.

God with Us

God with us at waking,
God with us at noontime,
God with us at evening,
God with us in sleeping.

God in us at waking,
God in us at noontime,
God in us at evening,
God in us in sleeping.

God's hands, our hands.
God's feet, our feet.
God's mouth, our mouth.
God's heart, our heart.

God's blessing, our blessing.
God's blessing, your blessing.
God's blessing, all blessings.
God's blessing, for all the world.

NOTES

Introduction

1. I blog at betharichardson.com.
2. John O'Donohue, *Anam Cara: A Book of Celtic Wisdom* (New York: HarperCollins, 1997), 92, 94.
3. *Carmina Gadelica: Hymns and Incantations*. With illustrative notes on words, rites, and customs, dying and obsolete: orally collected in the Highlands and islands of Scotland and translated into English by Alexander Carmichael. All three volumes of the work are available online at the National Library of Scotland at http://archive.org/details/nationallibraryofscotland. Search by "Carmina Gadelica." I have used prayers from these collections throughout this book and have taken the liberty to adapt the language.
4. Alexander Carmichael, *Carmina Gadelica: Hymns and Incantations*, I (Edinburgh: T. and A. Constable, 1900), 2–3.
5. Ibid., 3.

ABOUT THE AUTHOR

Grandpa Tom, Beth, mom Marty, and brother Charlie

BETH A. RICHARDSON is an ordained deacon in the Rocky Mountain Conference of The United Methodist Church serving as The Upper Room managing editor of *Alive Now* magazine and *Weavings: A Journal of the Christian Spiritual Life.*

Beth is the author of two Advent books: *Child of the Light* (Upper Room Books, 2006) and *The Uncluttered Heart* (Upper Room Books, 2009).

Beth received her master of divinity degree from Vanderbilt Divinity School in Nashville, Tennessee. A native Oklahoman and preacher's kid, she is a musician, worship leader, photographer, cartoonist, and writer.

Beth has the honor of sharing her life with Jack, a very wise Scottish terrier who blogs at jackthescottie.com.

Beth blogs at betharichardson.com.

for those who hunger for deep spiritual experience . . .

THE ACADEMY FOR SPIRITUAL FORMATION is an experience of disciplined Christian community emphasizing holistic spirituality—nurturing body, mind, and spirit. The program, a ministry of The Upper Room, is ecumenical in nature and includes both lay and clergy persons. Each Academy fosters spiritual rhythms—of study and prayer, silence and liturgy, solitude and relationship, rest and exercise. With offerings of both Two-Year and Five-Day models, Academy participants rediscover Christianity's rich spiritual heritage through worship, learning, and fellowship. The Academy's commitment to an authentic spirituality promotes balance, inner and outer peace, holy living and justice living—God's shalom.

Faculty trained in the wide breadth of Christian spirituality and practice provide content and guidance at each session of The Academy. Academy faculty presenters come from seminaries, monasteries, spiritual direction ministries, and pastoral ministries or other settings and are from a variety of traditions. Beth is an alumnus of the Two-Year Academy and has served on Five-Day Academy leadership teams.

The ACADEMY RECOMMENDS program seeks to highlight content that aligns with The Academy's mission to provide resources and settings where pilgrims encounter the teachings, sustaining practices, and rhythms that foster attentiveness to God's Spirit and therefore help spiritual leaders embody Christ's presence in the world.

Learn more at

academy.upperroom.org